THE WONDERFUL WORLD OF WEARABLE DEVICES

JENNIFER A. SWANSON

rosen publishing's
rosen central

New York

T0017111

Published in 2015 by The Rosen Publishing Group, Inc.
29 East 21st Street, New York, NY 10010

Copyright © 2015 by The Rosen Publishing Group, Inc.

First Edition

Library of Congress Cataloging-in-Publication Data

Swanson, Jennifer A., author.
The wonderful world of wearable devices/Jennifer A. Swanson.—First edition.
    pages cm.—(Digital and information literacy)
Includes bibliographical references and index.
ISBN 978-1-4777-7938-5 (library bound)—ISBN 978-1-4777-7939-2 (pbk.)—ISBN 978-1-4777-7940-8 (6-pack)
1. Wearable computers—Juvenile literature. 2. Biomedical engineering—Juvenile literature. 3. Technological innovations—Juvenile literature. I. Title. II. Series: Digital and information literacy.
QA76.592.S93 2015
303.48'3—dc23
                                                              2014007508

CONTENTS

INTRODUCTION

In this fast-paced world, people want information quickly. The need to stay connected via wireless gadgets is strong. But there are times when using a mobile phone or laptop becomes too challenging or is socially unacceptable. Enter the wearable device. Do you want to keep track of your heart rate while you work out? That is not a problem. There's a watch that can do that task for you. Have you ever seen a movie and wished you could have the same cool electronic gadgets that the character used? Well you don't have to wait anymore; that time is here. A company has developed Jarvis, an earphone headset system that responds to verbal commands and questions.

What makes a wearable device different from a mobile phone or laptop? A wearable device is exactly that—a device that you wear. It is a computer-operated device that is attached to or worn directly on the user. The gadget can be displayed on the wrist, arm, or waist. It may be a pair of glasses, a headset, or even a tiny bud that is inserted into the ear. The essential part is that the device has to be in contact with the body.

The idea behind wearable devices is simple. Each apparatus uses tiny sensors to collect data and record any interactions a user has throughout the day. The data is processed and uploaded to the Internet via a mobile phone, laptop, or cloud computing (the "cloud"). Finally, the data is presented as meaningful output to the user. The user takes the output and uses it to identify

With a fitness wearable device, people can now know exactly how many calories they burn during their daily bicycle rides.

his or her behavior and make modifications if necessary. For example, take a person who wants to lose weight. Increasing activity is a great way to get physically fit. But what if the person doesn't have time to go to the gym? Users with a wearable device, such as the Fitbit wristband, can track the number of steps they take per day. They can even see how their heart rate was affected. The Fitbit will process the information and report the results to the user. It may even give an enthusiastic response, such as a smiley face or comment. This motivation will keep the user walking, which in turn, will help him or her to lose weight.

Wearable devices are being met with skepticism by some and enthusiasm by others. Some say they are too bulky, complicated to use, and unattractive. Others can't wait to try out the latest gadgets. As with any new technology, there are problems. Security concerns, privacy issues, and battery life are all issues still needing to be solved. Despite the problems, wearable gadgets are here to stay. In fact, many see them as the next big thing in technology. Gartner, Inc., a world leader in information technology research, estimates that more than thirty million people will own and use a wearable device by 2020. Although embracing new technology sometimes might seem scary, being educated about the technology can help a person accept it. Learning how a device is created, and how it compiles and distributes data, is a great way to determine if a wearable device is beneficial to you.

Chapter 1

Wearing Your Computer

The idea for compact electronic devices isn't exactly new. It has been around for decades. Some early wearable devices were designed into watches. The first compact electronic wrist device was the algebraic calculator watch. It not only told time, but it could also add, subtract, multiply, and divide numbers. It could even perform complicated algebraic functions. Of course, not all wearable devices were for helping with math. Some gadgets focused instead on providing comfort and care for others.

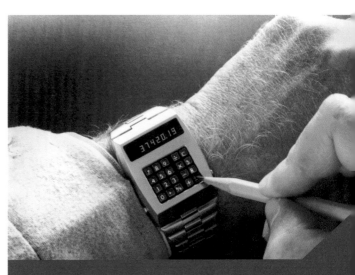

The Hughes Aircraft Company made a digital combination calculator and watch around 1974. It had a light-emitting diode (LED) display.

File   Edit   View   Favorites   Tools   Help

GIVING SIGHT TO PEOPLE WHO ARE BLIND OR VISUALLY IMPAIRED

GIVING SIGHT TO PEOPLE WHO ARE BLIND OR VISUALLY IMPAIRED

Developed in 1977 by C. C. Collins of the Smith-Kettlewell Eye Research Institute, the first wearable camera was created to help people who are blind or visually impaired distinguish shapes. It had a headset that held a 5-pound (2.27-kilogram) camera in place over one eye. The camera took visual images and converted them into a pressure signal. The signal was sent to a 1,024-point tactile grid placed on a vest. When an object appeared in front of the person, a sensor on the vest was activated. The sensor would apply pressure to the vest. When the person wearing the vest felt the pressure, he or she would know that something was in his or her path.

With recent advancements in technology, today's wearable devices are less bulky and easier to use than their predecessors. The Argus device, developed by a company called Second Sight, uses camera-mounted sunglasses containing a digital chip to transmit information to sensors that have been implanted in the retina of a person who is visually impaired. The sensors stimulate the retinal cells, which send impulses to the person's optic nerve. The optic nerve then sends them to the part of the brain that puts the impulses together as an image. The process enables the individual to perceive some aspect of images and movement, thus improving the person's ability to maneuver around objects.

Not a Cell Phone

Wearable devices are not cell phones, laptops, or even tablets. What makes them different? A wearable device contains sensors and scanners that continuously monitor the individual user. Some wearable devices even have their own computer processing unit (CPU), hard drive, power supply, and input/output devices. They are able to communicate with the user and other wireless devices.

How They Work

A wearable device is in constant contact with its user. For example, a device that monitors a person's health might keep track of the amount of energy he or she expended, the calories the individual ate, and his or her sleep patterns. The device takes in all the information. It then uploads the data wirelessly to a storage facility. The data can be sent over a Wi-Fi, Bluetooth, or mobile phone network. The data is then processed and retransmitted to the user. Some wearable devices have small visual displays so that the user can see data immediately. Others require the user to interact with an application (app) on his or her smartphone or laptop. The idea is that a wearable device provides a "hands-free" interaction with a computer. The user is encouraged to interact with the device as often as possible so that data can be exchanged and used.

A portable device is designed to receive information constantly. Many users never take their device off or even turn it off. Where does all that data go? Usually, if you want to save data, you save it on your personal computer. But many wearable devices, such as Google Glass, a product that consists of a headset and eyeglasses to capture data from a surrounding area, are being designed to upload data to the cloud. Cloud computing refers to the idea of storing data on the Internet itself, not a personal computer's hard drive. The cloud is accessed via a wireless connection and keeps your information close to you. Using the cloud to store data means that you can access the data from almost anywhere. This easy access is

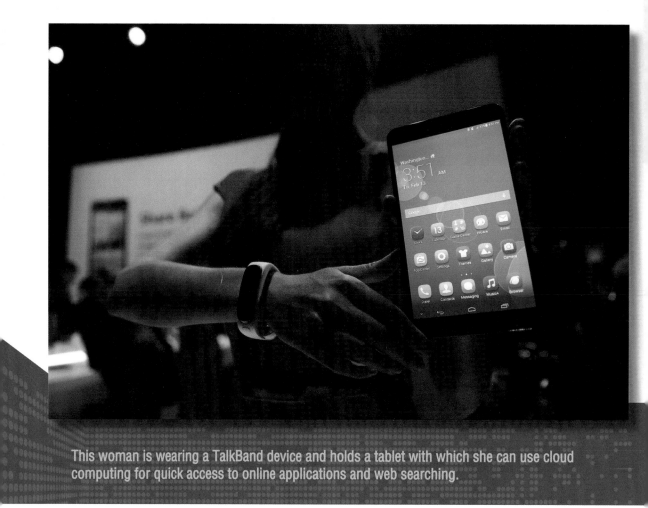

This woman is wearing a TalkBand device and holds a tablet with which she can use cloud computing for quick access to online applications and web searching.

exactly why wearable device manufacturers are using the cloud for data storage and retrieval. A person wearing a portable computer does not want to have to wait for the data but wants it immediately. The cloud delivers it by synchronizing data effortlessly whenever you need it.

Location, Location, Location

Where the portable device is worn is as important as how it operates. Hands-free units that allow ease of movement are the best type of

File   Edit   View   Favorites   Tools   Help

DEVICE-DRIVEN DATA

DEVICE-DRIVEN DATA

The amount of data collected from one wearable device is very large. Now imagine thousands of these data-mining devices, all depositing information on the Internet. Just how much data is that? According to the International Data Corporation (IDC), "By 2020 the digital universe will reach 40 zettabytes (ZB) [1 ZB = 1 billion terabytes (TB)], which is 40 trillion GB [gigabytes] of data, or 5,200 GB of data for every person on Earth." IDC estimates that by 2030, there will be 150 sensors per person on the planet. As reported by data scientist Nicholas Gonzalez, every sixty seconds, sensors are tracking the following:

- 98,000 tweets
- 695,000 Facebook status updates
- 11 million instant messages
- 698,445 Google Searches
- 168 million e-mails sent
- 1,820 TB of data
- 217 new mobile web users

portable devices. The wrist is a popular place for a wearable device because it is an easily accessible part of the body. It is convenient for repeated checking of data. Other places on the body, such as the ankle, head, eyes, chest, or even the waist are also great places for wearing a portable computer. The key consideration for placement has to do with the weight of the object. If the device weighs less than 1 pound (0.45 kg), it can rest easily on the wrist. A device weighing 2 pounds (0.91 kg) or more, however, is too heavy for the wrist. It should be located on a belt around the waist. The placement at the waist will be more comfortable for the user.

Wearable computers need to be made of strong and durable, but lightweight, material. They should be able to withstand shocks and vibrations and preferably be waterproof. Basically, the device needs to be able to hold up under any type of vigorous activity. Antibacterial or bacteria-resistant material is also desirable because commercial devices may have more than one user. Ergonomics, the science of making things comfortable, should

This device, called the Ring, manufactured by Logbar, is designed to allow the user to turn on appliances, access mobile phones, and even sign electronic checks, all with the wave of a finger.

definitely be taken into account. Wristbands or watches need to fit the curve of the body so that they are comfortable. A wearable device that causes discomfort will not be used.

Battery Life

Every electronic device requires a power source. Wearable devices do, too. But their power source needs to be compact and capable of operating continuously. To be useful, the devices need to have little or no downtime. Light, long-lasting battery power is preferred by most

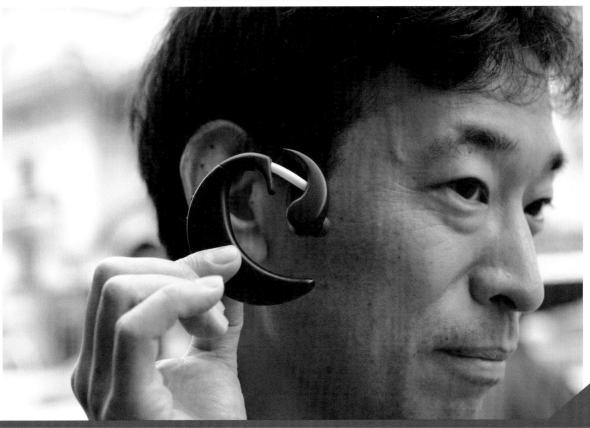

Many earpieces have quick-charging or rechargeable batteries so that the gadget remains available for user access and operation. This particular device is equipped with a GPS, compass, gyro-sensor, barometer, speaker, microphone, and Bluetooth wireless communication. It is controlled by facial expressions, including eye blinking.

13

people. Many wearable devices use lithium batteries that have a long life and are easily recharged. The batteries are designed to perform at peak efficiency. That means the devices can be programmed to use less energy throughout the day. The wrist device Zypad, made by the company Eurotech, has a sequencing mode that controls the battery usage. The computer can move from switch on, to standby, to suspend, to wake-up. Each stage has a different power requirement. In addition, the device can be powered completely off by manually pressing a button. The more comfortable and easy a device is to use and wear, the more desirable it will become to the user.

MYTH Wearable devices are just an extension of a smartphone.

FACT Wearable computing extends far beyond the simple Bluetooth capability of smartphones. The devices are embedded in shoes and clothing; one device was developed to be implanted in a person's tooth. Wearable technology is even being used to create BioStamp tags that attach directly to the skin to retrieve data from your body.

MYTH Wearable devices are difficult to recharge and require bulky power supply cords.

FACT Many wearable devices already use a special charging pad for repowering batteries. The device is simply placed on the pad, with no wiring required, and the battery is recharged as it lays there. Battery manufacturer LG Chem has created curved batteries that fit more easily into ergonomic devices and claims to provide up to 16 percent more power than traditional batteries.

MYTH Wearable devices are safe from computer hackers.

FACT Like all wireless products, wearable devices may be subject to breaches of security from computer-savvy hackers. Information stored on the cloud or transmitted via wireless communication remains fairly easy to access from outside sources. Even supposedly secure devices are capable of being hacked. Companies continue to direct additional monetary resources into research and development to create security measures for their devices.

Chapter 2

Personal vs. Professional Applications

hy is there so much excitement over wearable devices? The widespread use of cell phones, tablets, and laptops makes them the logical next step in technology. These mobile devices are intended to aid a person in all aspects of life, both personal and professional.

Keeping Fit

The most well-known and widely used wearable devices track health and fitness. Fitness gadgets include the Fitbit Flex, Jawbone Up, and the Amiigo. They offer ways to monitor a person's activity level and sleeping patterns, and they can even track heart rate and calculate calories burned per day. Each device sports different features and capabilities. They are all designed to be worn twenty-four hours a day, every day.

The Fitbit Flex is a sleek, rubber-like band that fits comfortably about the wrist. It offers users a way to not only track their fitness workouts, but also to keep tabs on their sleep patterns. The internal accelerometer keeps count of how many steps a person takes every day. When users input their height, weight, and age, the Flex calculates how many calories they burned per day. The ergonomic design allows the band to rest comfortably on the wrist. It is completely waterproof, so a user can wear it in the bath or shower. The sensors inside the Fitbit Flex also track the length and quality of the individual's sleep. It can tell how many times a person woke up during the night and how long he or she was awake.

The Jawbone Up has many of the same characteristics as the Fitbit Flex, but it also provides a few more. For example, it allows the user to set goals throughout the day for walking, sleeping, and eating. The Jawbone Up can supposedly sense a person's mood. By tapping on the smiley face icon, a sensor seems to read how the individual is feeling. Mood ranges go from "Totally Done" to "Amazing." Unlike the Fitbit Flex, the Jawbone Up enables an individual to interact socially with other Up users. Up owners simply search for other Up friends and can exchange information with them.

The Amiigo is a newly designed fitness tracker that consists of two parts: a waterproof polyurethane band that attaches to the

The Jawbone Up links wirelessly to a tablet or cell phone and can summarize the week's workouts for users so that they may see how far they have walked.

wrist and a shoe clip. Both the wristband and shoe clip have Bluetooth capability, which allows them to communicate information to an application on an iOS or Android cell phone. This revolutionary device allows for the wristband to capture movement of the upper body, while the shoe clip records lower body movement. The combination of the two devices enables actions such as cycling, leg exercises, and cross-training to be more accurately recorded because both the upper and lower bodies are being assessed. The sensors inside the device track heart rate, movement, percent of oxygen saturation, and number of calories burned. Users can view their fitness data, set goals, and enter challenges for themselves. They can also use it to track their sleep. Amiigo expects to hit the market in mid-2014 and is already doing quite well in presales.

File   Edit   View   Favorites   Tools   Help

THE NFL AND THE NBA

THE NFL AND THE NBA

The National Football League (NFL) and the National Basketball Association (NBA) use wearable devices to track their players during practices. NBA athletes wear a small device, about the size of a cell phone, on the inside of their jerseys. Positioned between their shoulder blades, the device records multidirectional movement and tracks their heart rate. Coaches can use this information to determine the fitness of each player and to review his performance. NFL teams use similar devices for their players, too. But the NFL is also investigating a new device called the X2 that will be installed in players' helmets. The X2 will monitor a player's brain waves, thus making it easier to determine if he has suffered a concussion and the severity of the injury.

The Buzz

What is so enticing about these wearable devices? Why do people feel the need to track their every movement? The theory is that making people aware of their activity—or lack thereof—will motivate them to move around more and stay fit. Walking ten thousand steps each day, eating healthy food, and getting eight hours of sleep every night are excellent ways to stay healthy. The wearable devices are designed to make the users aware of their habits and get them to change the bad ones. For people to understand their daily routines, the device must be able to compile and display the data in a simple manner. All the fitness devices have a USB port to allow for interface with either a cell phone or laptop. They also have mobile apps that sync real-time data with stored data to provide long-term feedback on daily and monthly goals. The Fitbit offers badges of encouragement when you reach your goals. It even gives you fun facts, such as "You climbed the tallest dinosaur" after you've walked ten thousand steps. The devices will also scold users if they don't meet their daily goals. The Jawbone Up will buzz and vibrate to let the user know that he or she has been inactive for too long.

Long-lasting batteries and easy charging make the interactive band a stress-free way of keeping people aware of their fitness levels. Besides wristbands, smartwatches and smartglasses are entering the wearable device market. Many smartwatches, such as the Pebble, not only track activity with built-in motion sensors, but also send notifications from a user's cell phone. The Nabu smartwatch, designed by gaming company Razer, can actually inform the user of an incoming phone call. The smartwatch has caller identity, so the user can tell who the call is from. The Cogito smartwatch, made by ConnecteDevice, shows snippets of text from e-mails, text messages, and even calendar posts. The short burst of information gives the user the ability to decide whether or not he or she really wants to reach into a pocket and pull out a cell phone to read the entire message. The Pebble smartwatch has its own applications that can be downloaded wirelessly from an Apple or Android app store. The watch can handle up to eight applications at a time.

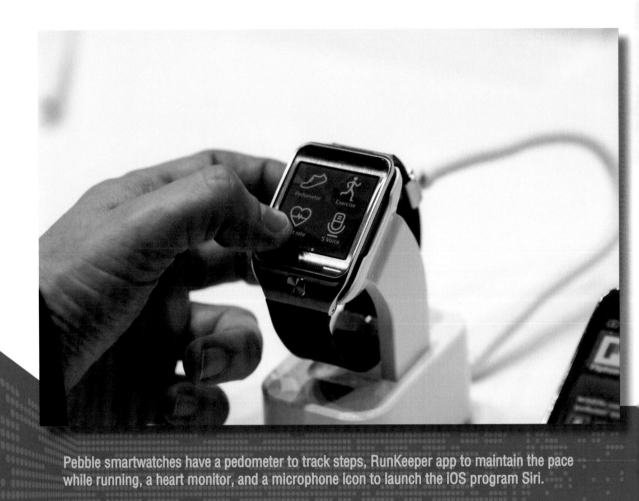

Pebble smartwatches have a pedometer to track steps, RunKeeper app to maintain the pace while running, a heart monitor, and a microphone icon to launch the iOS program Siri.

These apps can include Yelp, foursquare, poker, plain text readers, or even checking sports scores on ESPN. Users enjoy Pebble for is buzzing notification signaling, incoming e-mails, texts, or phone calls.

It's All About Style

If these wearable fitness devices are so easy to use and offer such great data, why doesn't everyone have them? The problem is fashion. In the past, many of the wearable devices available were fairly bulky, uncomfortable,

File   Edit   View   Favorites   Tools   Help

DISNEY MAGIC BANDS

DISNEY MAGIC BANDS

The Walt Disney Company has created Magic Bands for its customers. The wristbands are equipped with radio frequency identification (RFID) transmitters. Guests are able to use the band as a hotel room key, a park ticket, and a credit card. When the band is touched to a device reader, information is transferred instantly to the Disney computer or cash register. Security is assured through a four-digit PIN that the user enters every time he or she uses the band. Magic Bands information may be accessed by users via their smartphone or laptop. They can use the app associated with the band to make dining reservations or set up special experiences throughout the park. Disney intends to use the information from the Magic Bands to help gauge park movement and the popularity of certain events.

and rather unappealing in appearance. Consumers were turned off by large, mechanical looking devices, which looked like some kind of techno-gadget. Smart wristbands were passable as fitness gear but were not so fashion-forward when teamed with a business suit or dress. Ill-fitting or unattractive gadgets do not entice the user to wear them. Without continuous use, the benefits of collecting data are lost. To combat this problem, many wearable device manufacturers are teaming up with jewelry designers. Computer chip manufacturer Intel has decided to seek advice from jewelry company Opening Ceremony. The companies plan to make a jewelry pendant with Bluetooth capability. Fitbit is joining forces with designer Tory Burch to produce a Fitbit necklace and bracelet. Smartwatches such

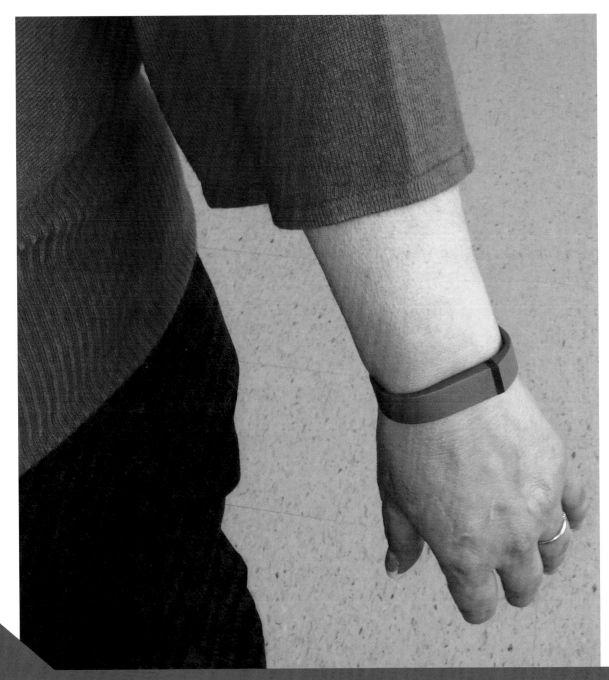

Fitbit offers ten different vibrant colors for its bands and styles them in a slim, sleek design so that they can complement any outfit.

as the Pebble have also introduced new devices that offer more high-end fashion. The Pebble Steel is available with a sporty leather band or a more fashionable black steel band similar in look to an expensive brand watch. The Samsung Gear 2 smartwatch allows users to swap out their bands for different styles and colors. Wearable device companies are hoping that improving the look of their products will bring new customers to them. If all goes well, the fashionable devices will encourage people to wear them for longer periods of time.

Keeping Track of Employees and Customers

Businesses are also jumping into the wearable device arena. Companies see the benefits of using wearable devices to collect data on their employees' habits. They are using badges, smartglasses, and wristbands to improve production. Special badges, such as the Hitachi Business Microscope, are worn on a lanyard around the neck by every employee. As the employees move about during the day, the sensors in the badges note how they move and interact with others. The sensors can even record the temperature and light in each room. When two employees come into contact, the badges communicate with each other. They record the interaction between the employees. The business leaders have access to the data from the devices. They review it and give feedback to employees on ways they can improve their workday plans. The goal is to increase harmony and productivity within the company.

Other companies are choosing a less personal approach when incorporating wearable devices. Vusix has developed smartglasses that are equipped with high-definition cameras. Designed to be used in warehouses and distribution centers, these smartglasses enable workers to scan the bar codes of the boxes they are handling. The devices tell the employees if the contents are fragile and need to be handled carefully. The smartglasses can even tell them if they have picked up the wrong box for shipping. The instant information provided by these smartglasses is extremely helpful. It helps the company maintain error-free shipping control. Not all companies are using

Smartglasses may become required equipment in manufacturing companies of the future. The real-time information and convenience of use make them an easy way to track materials and products.

wearable devices internally. Some businesses have created wearable devices to gather advertising and marketing information.

Wearable devices are becoming widespread in all aspects of business. The data gathered by these mobile computers and applications is being used to improve productivity, increase efficiency, and even target marketing and advertising. According to a survey conducted by Cornerstone OnDemand and Kelton Global Research Company, "Over 58 percent of workers would use wearable tech if it helped them do their job better."

Chapter 3

The Pros and Cons of Wearable Devices

The thought of wearing a computer on your body is appealing to some. They see the advantages of having immediate access to useable information about themselves and their workplaces. Others find the thought of a wearable device completely unpleasant. The idea of transmitting personal information across a fairly easily accessible wireless network is frightening. What if their information is hacked? What if their device is stolen? How much will it cost? It can be challenging to decide whether or not a wearable device will be helpful or harmful.

Going to School with Wearable Devices

Although wearable devices are taking off in the areas of personal fitness and business, educational institutions are not as quick to adopt this type of technology. The main reason for the delay may be the cost of wearable devices. Most schools are subject to pretty tight budget constraints. But others argue that the right wearable device for education has not yet become available. Devices that track health and fitness levels and distribution chains are not useful to the average student. Teachers want technology that will help them reach their students. They want to promote interaction and discussion. They do not want distraction in their classes. Google Glass might be one way to encourage beneficial academic experiences with wearable devices.

Google Glass in Action

Google has created a revolutionary wearable device. Called Google Glass, it is a pair of eyeglasses that act as a mobile camera and computer. The eyeglasses are specially designed to hold the basic parts of a smartphone. The tiny pieces of technology consist of a processor, 16 gigabytes of storage, a Bluetooth connection, and a miniature battery. The user interacts with the device via a small mounted screen, called a prism display, attached to the upper-right part of the eyeglasses near the right temple. The screen is connected to the Internet via a smartphone operating system, such as Android or iOS (Apple). Next to the screen is a camera that can take photos and videos.

Google Glass provides access to information instantly and is greatly beneficial to those businesses, such as airlines, that need to provide immediate assistance to their customers.

File   Edit   View   Favorites   Tools   Help

BRING YOUR OWN TECHNOLOGY

BRING YOUR OWN TECHNOLOGY

Some schools have tested a "bring your own technology" (BYOT) system, where students can bring their handheld devices to school. For the most part, these devices consist of smartphones, laptops, and tablets. But other schools are allowing their students to bring wearable devices such as smart-watches and headsets. The idea is that students, particularly ones who might have a learning disability, will benefit from the interaction a wearable device offers. Innovative teachers looking to incorporate wearable devices in the classroom are turning to blogs, such as the *Innovation Educator* (http://theinnovativeeducator.blogspot.com), for tips and ideas on how to integrate these devices into coursework.

Google Glass is controlled primarily through voice commands. The right temple of the eyeglasses is sensitive to touch, so it responds to that. To activate Google Glass, you simply tip your head back or tap on the right temple part of the eyeglasses. Google Glass can be used to take videos, read e-mails or text messages, and accept incoming phone calls. But what makes Google Glass so appealing to teachers?

Teachers can use the devices to take their students on a virtual tour. For example, one instructor, wearing his Google Glass device, went to the Louvre museum in Paris, France. As he walked past a painting, his students, back in their classroom in the United States, were able to see the painting, too. The instructor then had a discussion with his students about the artwork. His voice carried easily through Google Glass, over

A medical student watches video on his tablet as a heart surgeon, who is wearing Google Glass, transmits the video live during an operation. Smartglasses can stream audio and video via the Internet thousands of miles away to classrooms or business meetings so that everyone can be involved in the presentation in real time.

the Internet, to the computer in the classroom. Google Glass can also send out information to a group quickly. Teachers can create programs for students to access and comment on. The device's uses are only now being discovered and applied to an education setting. To some teachers, the benefits of Google Glass seem amazing. Other teachers, though, see wearable devices as nothing more than a classroom distraction.

File   Edit   View   Favorites   Tools   Help

GOOGLE GLASS'S UNEXPECTED PRIVACY BACKLASH

GOOGLE GLASS'S UNEXPECTED PRIVACY BACKLASH

Users of Google Glass are encountering unexpected criticism from the public. Total strangers who object to being videoed are confronting them. Because there isn't a visible indication of whether or not the Google Glass video is recording, people who believe they are being recorded without their permission are becoming angry. They feel uncomfortable with technology they can't control. In fact, some restaurants are already beginning to ban the devices completely. This ban might be challenging to accomplish because some users have the device installed on their prescription eyeglasses. It will take time and education for people to accept this new technology.

Invasion of Privacy

Wearable gadgets that are active twenty-four hours a day collect huge amounts of personal data. Most devices, however, don't store the data themselves. They upload it to an app on a smartphone or laptop. The data is transmitted via the cloud, Bluetooth, or Wi-Fi. Hackers have been known to access the information being transmitted wirelessly. What if you lose your wearable device? Will someone be able to access the information? The answer is, yes, a hacker might be able to access your data. Although smartphones and laptops have programs to encrypt and secure information, many wearable devices do not. Make sure to check the device before purchasing it to see what type of security measures, if any, the manufacturer offers. With the explosion of identity theft today, many companies are beginning to address the problem of security and privacy on their devices. For example, the Intel Corporation, which owns the McAfee brand of security programs, plans to use McAfee mobile security products on its new wearable devices.

Companies see the benefits from mobile computing, such as improving safety, enhancing products, and increasing productivity. Yet devices that track and record your every movement can be intimidating. Some would even consider them invasive. What if you get into a disagreement with a coworker? If your boss monitors your device output, he or she may find out. What if you decide to have a day free from exercise? The same wearable device that offers you encouragement for meeting your daily walking goal could scold you for taking a day of rest. Who needs that? No one wants to have to be aware of everything they say and do every minute of the day. People also do not want to have computers making them feel guilty about choices they have made.

Google Glass Is Banned On These Premises

stopthecyborgs.org ⊛⊕⊜⊖

Not every business is embracing Google Glass. Some restaurants, movie theaters, and casinos are banning Google Glass because of privacy issues for their customers and to prevent movie piracy and cheating.

Joanna Pfahler is a content marketing specialist at MSI Data, which is a company that provides workforce automation software and is creating apps for wearable devices. Pfahler recommends that employers do the following so that they don't upset their employees while trying to benefit from these workplace technologies:

- "Let users know in advance what's being tracked and analyzed
- Make sure it's clear that managers only aggregate data and don't see statistics for individual analysis
- Make participation optional
- Link company goals with individual goals
- Emphasize common goals like safety and improved performance over evaluation and efficiency"

The final recommendation is to have an opt-out option, if possible. This choice means that the employee or customer can simply say no to wearing the device. Forcing technology on people rarely results in a happy workplace. It is better to back off and let people understand what is happening first, then reintroduce the product at a later date.

Making Your Own Wearable Device

Of course, not everyone is put off by wearable device technology. There are those individuals who embrace it with open arms. In fact, they are so interested that they want to create their own wearable device. Development kits are being constructed so that users can make their own wearable devices. The company Freescale Semiconductor created the Wearable Reference Platform (WaRP) kit, which contains sensors and processors that individual designers can put together to produce smartwatches, smartglasses, and activity and sports trackers. Raspberry Pi, a tiny fully operational computer, is also being used by tech-savvy individuals to create wearable device computers. Intel has developed the smallest computer available. Called Edison, it is the size of a standard secure digital (SD) card typically used in a camera. Edison is the perfect size to fit into many small wearable devices.

TEN GREAT QUESTIONS
TO ASK A WEARABLE DEVICE DEVELOPER

1 What type of operating systems does the device use?

2 How does an individual user interact with the device?

3 What type of feedback does the user get from the device?

4 How does the information received from the device help the user?

5 How much does the wearable device cost?

6 Can multiple wearable devices interact with one another?

7 What is the typical battery life for the wearable device?

8 How is the battery inside the wearable device recharged?

9 Who can users contact if they have problems with the wearable device?

10 How prevalent do you think your wearable device will become in the future?

Chapter 4

The High-Tech Future

The future of wearable devices has already arrived. Every month, new mobile computing gadgets with the latest wearable technology are hitting the market. Head-mounted displays, "smart" computers that learn, and high-tech medical devices are just a few of the benefits offered by wearable devices.

Mobile Gaming

Although the biggest growth area for wearable devices is in health and fitness, the realm of mobile gaming isn't far behind. Internet and video games are hugely popular with people of all ages. Google Glass is the premier device in head-mounted display (HMD) technology. HMD is a computer system that is worn on the head. It typically has some type of display that a person looks through and can interact with the computer. HMDs such as those used in Google Glass may be an ideal platform for playing a video game. In fact, Google has already created the first game for its Glass device. It is called *Global Food Fight* and users can play the game as they walk. Microsoft has

Wearable devices for gaming systems are a big draw for the avid gamer. They allow the users to experience a video game in a 3D virtual simulation, as if they were actually inside the game.

created its Fortaleza Glasses for use with the Xbox gaming system. The eyeglasses enable the wearer to see and experience the game in three-dimensional (3D) virtual reality. The eyeglasses are also capable of connecting to the Internet and smartphones that have fourth-generation (4G) connectivity.

"Smart" Technology for Medicine

People with chronic illnesses and medical issues may be the ones to benefit most from wearable devices. Tiny monitors capable of tracking specific health issues and alerting individuals to changes will be the kinds of devices needed the most. Already gadgets exist that can monitor pain levels, glucose levels, and insulin levels, and track vital signs. Devices can monitor brain waves and even take electrocardiograms of the heart. All this information is transmitted wirelessly to an individual's doctor. People that have conditions such as kidney disease, diabetes, or heart problems consider these devices very beneficial. The devices ease the stress of self-monitoring and offer more chance for people to decrease their reliance on other individuals.

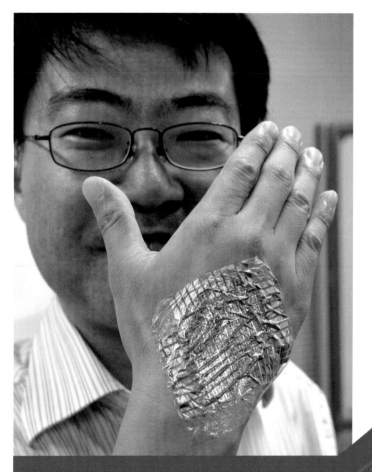

BioStamps, such as this one, are not only able to track and monitor body functions, but may also soon verify a person's identity for accessing mobile computers and the cloud.

Tattoos with a Medical Purpose

MC10, a high-performance electronics company, has created an electronic circuit technology called the BioStamp. A BioStamp is an electronic device that is worn directly on the skin. It contains sensors that can track blood pressure, heart rate, hydration levels, and even body temperature. Information is sent via a wireless network to a person's doctor. The tiny BioStamp sits on a biodegradable adhesive strip. It is applied directly to the skin, just like a

File   Edit   View   Favorites   Tools   Help

ACCESS FOR EVERYONE

ACCESS FOR EVERYONE

Wearable devices usually carry very high price tags. When it was made available for a one-day limited promotional purchase, Google Glass cost around $1,500 for one pair of eyeglasses. Many devices are so new that they haven't hit the market yet and their prices haven't been set. But analysts speculate that the cost of medical wearable devices may be high. Who is going to pay for these devices? The answer might be medical insurance companies. Google has struck a deal with VSP, a major optical health insurer, for VSP to cover frames and prescription lenses for Google Glass wearers. Prior to this agreement, people who wore prescription lenses had to wear Google Glass over their own eyeglasses or keep switching back and forth. Now people who need to wear eyeglasses can use Google Glass with their very own prescription lenses. Will other insurance companies follow this model? It's hard to say. But if one company offers coverage, then consumers will definitely want them all to do so.

temporary tattoo or an adhesive bandage. The flexibility of the electronic stamp allows it to move seamlessly with its user. Are you heading to the gym to work out? That is not a problem because the stamp moves with you and can communicate not only with your doctor's office, but also with your smartphone. Each BioStamp lasts approximately two weeks.

The technology in the BioStamp is also being used to create head impact projectors. A product from Reebok and MC10 is called the Checklight. It is a small stretchy cap that is worn on the head, similar to a swim cap. It can also be worn under a helmet. The tiny sensors inside the cap track any blows to the head and the number of hits a person has taken.

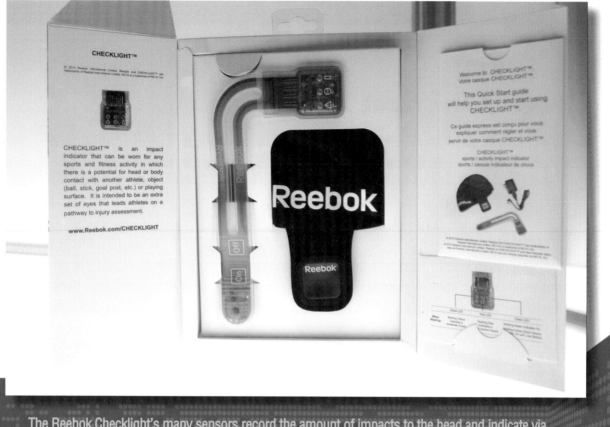

The Reebok Checklight's many sensors record the amount of impacts to the head and indicate via lights in the back when a blow has been received. A red light means the person has taken a hard blow and should be checked for a concussion.

The Checklight also gives information on whether a person has suffered a concussion and how severe that injury is. The NFL is looking into making it mandatory for all its athletes to wear one of these devices to gather impact data while they are playing.

Wearable Devices for the Long Term

The hype surrounding wearable devices is almost at fever pitch. The benefits offered by the new technology seem limitless and, for many people,

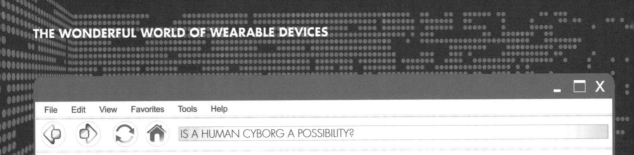

File   Edit   View   Favorites   Tools   Help

IS A HUMAN CYBORG A POSSIBILITY?

IS A HUMAN CYBORG A POSSIBILITY?

You've seen them in movies. Remember the beings that are half-human and half-machine? They are called cyborgs. They wear cool glasses and have bits of metal attached to their bodies. They act like humans but think and react with the speed of computers. With the assistance of wearable devices, is the existence of a cyborg a reality? It is unlikely, although some argue that combining Google Glass with the MC10 BioStamp technology is sort of like creating a cyborg. That is probably stretching the truth. The BioStamps are made of thin silicon. Google Glass is a tiny computer worn on eyeglasses. Together, these two devices hardly add up to create a cyborg. Still, it is an interesting question. Will there be cyborgs in the future? What do you think?

really cool. But companies interested in being in the wearable device sector for the long haul need to be cautious. According to Dara Kerr's article on wearable devices, J. P. Gownder, vice president and principal analyst at Forrester Research, offers the following three factors for companies to make their prime concerns:

- Create a device that can access multiple services, such as the cloud, iOS, and Android operating systems.
- Be sure that the wearable device is compatible with existing businesses and that they will support it. One example would be encouraging hospitals to hand out and monitor fitness and health devices.

- The trend for new wearable devices should reflect customer interest. That means there should be a focus on creating new devices in the areas of health, fitness, security, and other workplaces that want to use them.

Like all new technology, it will take time for the public to embrace wearable devices. After all, if you had told people in the 1990s that in twenty years they would be walking around talking on their mobile phones, would they have believed you? Probably not. Now mobile phones are so much more than phones. They allow individuals to text, read, send e-mail, and stay connected via social networks. Most people can't imagine life without a smartphone. Who knows what type of technology the wearable devices will be capable of in the future? It's possible that the teenagers of the 2030s won't even know what a smartphone is. Their jewelry or clothing may house their Internet connection, which they can access by a simple wave or touch of their hand. Google Glass may not only allow people to access the Internet as they walk, but also give them a peek into their techno-logical future.

GLOSSARY

aggregate data Data elements from different sources that are collected and combined.

Android operating system A system based on the Linux kernel and designed primarily for touchscreen mobile devices, such as smartphones and tablet computers.

BioStamp A flexible, wearable electronic circuit worn on the skin like a temporary tattoo, designed by John Rogers of MC10 and the University of Illinois.

Bluetooth A wireless technology standard for exchanging data over short distances via radio frequencies.

central processing unit (CPU) The computer hardware that carries out the instructions from the user. It is the brain of the computer.

cyborg Also called a "cybernetic organism," it is a being with both organic and mechanical parts.

ergonomic Describing an object to which efficient and comfortable design and arrangement have been applied.

input/output The communication between a computer (input) and a person or other outside influence (output).

invasive Tending to infringe or intrude on a person's thoughts or privacy.

iOS A mobile operating system designed and used by Apple, Inc.

lanyard A cord or strap to hold something, such as an identity card, around the neck.

radio frequency identification (RFID) The wireless use of radio-frequency electromagnetic fields to transfer data.

SD card Secure digital memory card for use with cell phones, digital cameras, and other mobile devices to record images.

smart technology Interactive devices that allow a user to input information from which the device can learn.

tactile grid A pressure sensor arranged in a grid-like pattern.

Wi-Fi Technology that allows an electronic device to exchange data or connect to the Internet wirelessly using radio waves.

FOR MORE INFORMATION

Canada.com Technology
365 Bloor Street East
Toronto, ON M4W 3L4
Canada
(800) 668-7678
Website: http://o.canada.com/category/technology
This site carries the latest information on up-to-date technological advances
     in Canada.

Consumer Electronics Association
1919 South Eads Street
Arlington, VA 22202
(866) 233-7968
Website: http://www.cesweb.org
The association tracks all of the consumer electronic shows across the
     world and displays the latest in computer technology.

Fitbit, Inc.
150 Spear Street
San Francisco, CA 94105
(877) 623-4997
Website: http://www.fitbit.com
This company offers information on all of its fitness band products.

Google, Inc.
1600 Amphitheatre Parkway
Mountain View, CA 94043
(650) 253-0000
Website: http://www.google.com/glass/start
The website offers information on Google Glass and how it works.

MIT Technology Review
P.O. Box 16327
North Hollywood, CA 91615-6327
(800) 877-5230
Website: http://www.technologyreview.com
Operated by a media company, this online magazine identifies important
    new technologies and explains their impact on society to determine
    how they will change people's lives.

Thalmic Labs
Thalmic Labs Special Projects Facility #3
24 Charles Street West
Kitchener, ON N2G 1H2
Canada
(888) 777-2546
Website: https://www.thalmic.com/en/myo
The lab's website contains all of the information about the Myo gesture
    control armband.

Websites

Because of the changing nature of Internet links, Rosen Publishing has developed
an online list of websites related to the subject of this book. This site is updated
regularly. Please use this link to access the list:

http://www.rosenlinks.com/DIL/Wear

FOR FURTHER READING

Berman, Neil, Mike Stanfield, Jason Rouse, and Joel Scambray. *Hacking Exposed Mobile Security Secrets & Solutions*. New York, NY: McGraw-Hill Publishing, 2013.

Duffy, Thomas. *Programming with Mobile Applications: Android(TM), iOS, and Windows Phone 7*. Independence, KY: Cengage Learning, 2012.

Gardner, Lyza Danger, and Jason Grigsby. *Head First Mobile Web* (Brain-Friendly Guides). Sebastopol, CA: O'Reilly Media, 2011.

Gargenta, Marko, and Masumi Nakamura. *Learning Android: Develop Mobile Apps Using Java and Eclipse*. Sebastopol, CA: O'Reilly Media, 2013.

Gerber, Larry. *Cloud-Based Computing* (Digital Information Literacy). New York, NY: Rosen Publishing, 2014.

Hartman, Kate. *Make: Wearable & Electronics: Tools and Techniques for Prototyping Interactive Wearables*. Sebastopol, CA: Maker Media, 2014.

Kamal, Devi. *Mobile Computing*. New York, NY: Oxford University Press, 2012.

Payton, Theresa, and Ted Claypoole. *Privacy in the Age of Big Data: Recognizing Threats, Defending Your Rights, and Protecting Your Family*. Washington, DC: Rowman & Littlefield Publishers, 2014.

Pogue, David. *iPhone: The Missing Manual*. Sebastopol, CA: O'Reilly Media, 2013.

Reid, Neil. *Wireless Mobility: The Why of Wireless*. New York, NY: McGraw-Hill Publishing, 2010.

Saylor, Michael. *The Mobile Wave: How Mobile Intelligence Will Change Everything*. New York, NY: Vanguard Press, 2012.

Ventura, Marne. *Google Glass and Robotics Innovator Sebastian Thrun*. Minneapolis, MN: Lerner Publishing, 2014.

Wilkinson, Colin. *Mobile Platforms: Getting Information on the Go*. New York, NY: Rosen Publishing, 2011.

Woodcock, Jon, and Chris Woodford. *Cool Stuff 2.0 and How It Works*. New York, NY: Dorling Kindersley, 2007.

Xu, Yangsheng, Wen Lung Li, and Ka Keung Li. *Intelligent Wearable Interfaces*. Hoboken, NJ: John Wiley & Sons, 2008.

BIBLIOGRAPHY

Beavis, Gareth. "A Cool Watch—but It's Already Been Outshone." April 14, 2014. Retrieved May 27, 2014 (http://www.techradar.com/reviews/gadgets/samsung-gear-2-1226993/review).

Best Fitness Tracker Reviews. "Amigo Fitness Bracelet Review." Retrieved May 27, 2014 (http://www.bestfitnesstrackerreviews.com/amiigo-fitness-tracker-review.html).

Bhas, Nitin. "The Evolution of Wearable Devices: Are They the Future?" JuniperResearch.com, September 2012. Retrieved January 9, 2014 (http://www.juniperresearch.com/analyst-xpress-blog/2012/11/02/the-evolution-of-wearable-devices-are-they-the-future).

Cornerstone OnDemand. "The State of the Workplace Report." August 2012. Retrieved February 1, 2014 (http://www.cornerstoneondemand.com/resources/research/state-of-workplace-productivity-2013).

Disney by the Numbers. "News: More Magic Band Information." February 6, 2013. Retrieved January 9, 2014 (http://www.disneybythenumbers.com/blog/blog_files/More%20Magic%20Band%20Information.html).

Gonzalez, Nicholas. "Big Data Analytics for Device-Driven Data Will Drive Even Bigger Change." WiredInnovationsInsights.com, August 22, 2013. Retrieved February 7, 2014 (http://insights.wired.com/profiles/blogs/big-data-analytics-for-device-driven-data#axzz2sf75B8ZC).

Gownder, J. P. "Wearables Will Reshape the Way Enterprises Work." ComputerWorld.com, November 18, 2013. Retrieved January 9, 2014 (http://www.computerworld.com.au/article/532133/wearables_will_reshape_way_enterprises_work).

Hernandez, Daniela. "New Wearable Device Helps Blind Patients See Shapes and Colors." Wired.com, August 6, 2013. Retrieved January 9, 2014 (http://www.wired.com/gadgetlab/2013/08/argus-bionic-retina).

Johnson, Dave. "Google Glass, Coming Soon to an Eyeglass Store Near You?" CBS.com, February 5, 2014. Retrieved February 7, 2014 (http://www.cbsnews.com/new/google-glass-becomes-more-practical-closer-to-reality).

Kerr, Dara. "Google Glass Accessories on the Way: Shades, Shields, Earbuds."
    CNET.com, October 30, 2013. Retrieved January 9, 2014 (http://
    news.cnet.com/8301-1023_3-57610127-93/google-glass-accessories
    -on-the-way-shades-shields-earbuds).

Kerr, Dara. "Wearables Expected to Graduate to 2.0 at CES 2014." CNET
    .com, January 6, 2014. Retrieved January 9, 2014 (http://news.cnet
    .com/8301-11386_3-57616730-76/wearables-expected-to-graduate
    -to-2.0-at-ces-2014).

Miller, Claire Cain. "Google Glass to Be Covered by Vision Care Insurer VSP."
    New York Times, January 28, 2014. Retrieved February 1, 2014 (http://
    www.nytimes.com/2014/01/28/technology/google-glass-to-be
    -covered-by-vision-care-insurer-vsp.html?ref=todayspaper&_r=1).

Pfahler, Joanna. "The New Business Attire: How Field Service Can Benefit from
    New Wearable Gadgets." MSIData.com, November 7, 2013. Retrieved
    February 1, 2014 (http://www.msidata.com/benefit-from-wearable
    -technology).

Reid, Neil. *Wireless Mobility: The Why of Wireless*. New York, NY: McGraw-
    Hill Publishing, 2010.

Talukder, Askoke, and Roopa Yavagal. *Mobile Computing: Technology,
    Applications and Service Creations*. New York, NY: Mc-Graw-Hill, 2007.

Tew, Sara. "Jawbone Up Review: An Easy-to-Wear and Insightful Fitness Pal."
    CNET.com, May 9, 2013. Retrieved February 7, 2014 (http://reviews
    .cnet.com/watches-and-writs-devices/jawbone-up/4505-3512
    _7-35536649.html).

TrendMicro.com. "Big Data, Wearable Devices Create Anxiety About Storage
    Practices." October 18, 2013. Retrieved January 9, 2014 (http://blog.
    trendmicro.com/big-data-wearable-devices-create-anxiety
    -storage-practices).

Wilson, James. "The Hot New Thing in Business Attire Is Technology."
    WallStreetJournal.com, October 20, 2013. Retrieved January 9, 2014
    (http://online.wsj.com/news/articles/SB4000142405270230379640
    4579099203059125112).

INDEX

About the Author

Jennifer A. Swanson has extensive knowledge of the Disney Magic Band wearable device because she lives near Orlando, Florida, and visits Disney World often. Swanson is the author of more than twenty books for young people. When not writing, she works as a middle school science instructor.

Photo Credits

Cover and p. 1 (from left) © iStockphoto.com/alexey boldin, © iStockphoto .com/mikkelwilliam, © iStockphoto.com/Chesky W, © iStockphoto.com/ ZooCat; p. 5 Colleen Proppe/Moment Mobile/flickr Editorial/Getty Images; p. 7 Underwood Photo Archives/SuperStock; p. 10 Bloomberg/Getty Images; p. 12 The Asahi Shimbun/Getty Images; pp. 13, 34, 35 Yoshikazu Tsuno/ AFP/Getty Images; p. 17 Lindsey Janich/Moment Mobile/flickr Editorial/ Getty Images; p. 20 Ivan Garcia/Shutterstock.com; p. 22 Denise Panyik-Dale/Moment Mobile/flickr Editorial/Getty Images; p. 24 Vuzix; p. 26 SN/ Landov; p. 28 © The Star-Ledger/Robert Sciarrino/The Image Works; p. 30 stopthecyborgs.org/google-glass-ban-signs/CC BY 3.0; p. 37 Joe Klamar/ AFP/Getty Images; cover and interior pages (dots graphic) © iStockphoto.com/ suprun; interior pages (browser window graphic) © iStockphoto.com/AF-studio.

Designer: Nicole Russo; Editor: Kathy Kuhtz Campbell